EVANGELINE DONALDSON

GIG WORK 101
A QUICKSTART GUIDE TO TURNING YOUR SIDE HUSTLE GOALS INTO REALITY

Copyright © 2024 by Evangeline Donaldson

All rights reserved. No part of this publication may be reproduced, stored or transmitted in any form or by any means, electronic, mechanical, photocopying, recording, scanning, or otherwise without written permission from the publisher. It is illegal to copy this book, post it to a website, or distribute it by any other means without permission.

Evangeline Donaldson asserts the moral right to be identified as the author of this work.

Evangeline Donaldson has no responsibility for the persistence or accuracy of URLs for external or third-party Internet Websites referred to in this publication and does not guarantee that any content on such Websites is, or will remain, accurate or appropriate.

Designations used by companies to distinguish their products are often claimed as trademarks. All brand names and product names used in this book and on its cover are trade names, service marks, trademarks and registered trademarks of their respective owners. The publishers and the book are not associated with any product or vendor mentioned in this book. None of the companies referenced within the book have endorsed the book.

First edition

This book was professionally typeset on Reedsy.
Find out more at reedsy.com

Contents

I YOU CAN DO THIS!

1	Introduction	3
2	Chapter 1: Understanding Gig Work	6
3	Chapter 2: Choosing Your Side Hustle (Types of Gig Jobs)	7
4	Chapter 3: Clarifying Your Goals and Objectives	11
5	Chapter 4: The Money Plan	14
6	Chapter 5: The Good, The Bad and the Challenging Aspects of...	20
7	Chapter 6: Work Smarter, Not Harder	28
8	Conclusion	30

I

YOU CAN DO THIS!

This book is your passport to the world of gig work—a overview that not only introduces you to the diverse landscape of gig opportunities but also empowers you to choose the path that resonates with your interests and ambitions.

1

Introduction

The Power of Side Hustles

In a rapidly changing world, where financial security can often feel like an elusive dream, the concept of a side hustle has emerged as a beacon of hope for countless individuals seeking to achieve their goals. Whether you dream of financial freedom, paying off debt, saving for a dream vacation, or even turning your passion into a full-time career, a side hustle can be the catalyst that propels you toward these aspirations. This book is your guide to understanding how a side hustle can help you reach your goals and how to harness its incredible potential.

The New Normal

Gone are the days when a traditional 9-to-5 job was the only pathway to financial stability. The landscape of employment has shifted dramatically, giving rise to what we now call the gig economy. This new normal offers a multitude of opportunities for individuals to create additional income streams through side hustles. In this era, where job security is no longer guaranteed and the cost of living continues to rise, a side hustle provides a safety net, a lifeline to financial resilience.

The Versatility of Side Hustles

The beauty of side hustles lies in their diversity. They come in various forms, catering to different skill sets, interests, and goals. Whether you have a knack for writing, graphic design, coding, or a passion for cooking, there's a side hustle waiting for you. From freelancing on platforms like Upwork and Fiverr to offering your services as a rideshare driver for Uber or Lyft, the possibilities are virtually endless.

Defining Your Goals

The journey to reaching your goals begins with a clear definition of what those goals are. Do you dream of paying off that student loan debt that's been weighing you down for years? Or perhaps you aspire to build an emergency fund to provide financial security for your family. Your goals could be as grand as starting your own business or as simple as affording a dream vacation. Whatever they may be, your side hustle can be tailored to align with your specific objectives.

The Power of Financial Freedom

One of the most compelling reasons people turn to secondary income sources is the promise of financial freedom. Imagine a life where you're not constrained by the limitations of your full time job. A side hustle can provide that financial breathing room, allowing you to save more, invest wisely, and break free from the paycheck-to-paycheck cycle. Financial freedom is not just a distant dream; it's an achievable reality, and your gig work can be your ticket to that destination.

Turning Passions into Profits

Perhaps you've always had a passion or a hobby that you've never considered as a potential source of income. The beauty of side hustles is that they offer you the opportunity to turn your passions into profits. Whether you love crafting, gardening, photography, or playing a musical instrument, there's a market for your talents and interests. This book will explore how to identify and leverage your passions to create a fulfilling and profitable financial cushion.

The Journey Ahead

In the chapters that follow, we will delve into the intricacies of the gig economy, exploring the various types of side hustles available to you and how to navigate them successfully. We will discuss the practical steps to set up your side hustle, manage your time effectively, and handle the financial aspects, including budgeting and tax considerations. You'll also gain insights into the potential challenges and pitfalls of side hustling and learn how to overcome them.

Ultimately, this book is your roadmap to realizing the incredible potential of side hustles in helping you reach your goals, both big and small. It's about taking control of your financial future, creating opportunities for yourself, and building a life that aligns with your dreams. So, let's embark on this journey together, and discover the transformative power of side hustles. Your goals are within reach, and your side hustle is the key to unlocking them.

2

Chapter 1: Understanding Gig Work

Gig work, often referred to as the gig economy, represents a dynamic and transformative shift in the way people earn a living. At its core, gig work involves individuals taking on short-term, flexible, and often independent contractor positions to earn income. Unlike traditional 9-to-5 jobs, gig work doesn't come with the constraints of a fixed schedule, a long-term commitment, or a single employer.

In the world of gig work, you become your own boss, with the freedom to choose when, where, and how you work. This flexibility is one of its defining characteristics, making it particularly appealing to those seeking to balance work with other life commitments.

Gig work spans a wide range of activities, from freelancing in creative fields like writing and graphic design to providing services such as ridesharing, food delivery, and task-based jobs like assembling furniture or dog walking. This chapter sets the stage for the exciting journey ahead, exploring the diverse landscape of gig work and its potential to reshape your career and lifestyle.

3

Chapter 2: Choosing Your Side Hustle (Types of Gig Jobs)

Freelancing Platforms: Unlocking Your Skills for Profit

In today's gig economy, freelancing platforms like Upwork and Fiverr have revolutionized the way individuals connect with clients, turning their skills and expertise into lucrative sources of income. These platforms offer a virtual marketplace where freelancers can offer their services to a global clientele, opening up a world of possibilities.

Upwork, for instance, is a vast ecosystem that caters to a multitude of skill sets, ranging from web development and content writing to graphic design and digital marketing. Freelancers create profiles, showcase their portfolios, and bid on projects posted by clients. On the other hand, Fiverr, known for its "gigs," allows freelancers to offer specific services at set prices, making it easier for clients to find what they need quickly.

The advantages of freelancing platforms are abundant. They provide a platform for talent to shine, connecting professionals with clients who require their expertise. Freelancers can set their rates, work on projects they're passionate about, and enjoy the flexibility of choosing their working hours.

However, competition can be fierce, and success on these platforms often relies on building a stellar reputation through client reviews and consistent, high-quality work. Whether you're a seasoned professional or just starting, freelancing platforms can be a gateway to fulfilling your financial goals and career aspirations.

Task-Based Platforms: Earning on Your Own Terms

Task-based platforms, exemplified by services like TaskRabbit and Gigwalk, offer an innovative way to earn money by completing short-term tasks or assignments. These platforms cater to a wide range of needs, from household chores to marketing research, and they empower individuals to monetize their time and skills effectively.

TaskRabbit, for instance, connects individuals and businesses with "Taskers" who can assist with everyday tasks such as furniture assembly, grocery shopping, or handyman services. Gigwalk, on the other hand, allows users to earn money by completing quick, location-based tasks like verifying store displays or taking photos for marketing purposes.

The allure of task-based platforms lies in their simplicity and versatility. Users can choose tasks that match their skills, interests, and schedules, making it an excellent option for those seeking a flexible side hustle. Plus, the ability to pick and choose assignments means you can earn money doing tasks you genuinely enjoy.

Task-based platforms provide a unique opportunity to earn income on your terms, offering a glimpse into the evolving landscape of the gig economy.

On the Road to Profits: Ride-Sharing and Delivery Services

CHAPTER 2: CHOOSING YOUR SIDE HUSTLE (TYPES OF GIG JOBS)

In the bustling gig economy, ride-sharing and delivery services have emerged as popular options for individuals looking to turn their vehicles into money-making machines. Companies like Uber, Lyft, DoorDash, and Shipt have disrupted traditional transportation and food delivery industries, offering opportunities for flexible earnings and a unique blend of independence and convenience. The sign-up is quite simple: apply online, pass a background check, and begin accepting orders to shop and deliver using the app at your convenience. You retain the autonomy to determine when you want to work. These types of services are typically fast-paced, and will keep you busy meeting the various needs of people in your community.

The Ride-Sharing Revolution

Ride-sharing services like Uber and Lyft have transformed the way people get from point A to point B. For those with a car and a desire to earn money, these platforms provide a chance to become a rideshare driver. The process is relatively straightforward: sign up, undergo a background check, and start accepting passengers through the app. As a driver, you have control over your working hours and can decide when and where to pick up passengers.

The appeal of ride-sharing is multifaceted. It's an excellent option for those who enjoy driving and meeting new people. It's also a highly accessible gig; as long as you have a vehicle and meet certain requirements, you can become a driver. Plus, earnings can be quite competitive, particularly during peak hours or in high-demand areas.

Delivering Delights: Food and Grocery Delivery Services

Food delivery services like DoorDash and grocery delivery platforms such as Shipt offer another dimension to gig work. These services cater to consumers' growing demand for convenience, enabling individuals to earn by delivering meals, groceries, or other essentials directly to customers' doorsteps.

DoorDash, for example, connects drivers (known as "Dashers") with local restaurants and allows them to deliver orders to hungry customers. Shipt, on the other hand, focuses on grocery shopping and delivery, allowing individuals to shop for and deliver groceries to clients' homes.

These platforms offer gig workers flexibility and diversity in their work. You can choose to work during lunch and dinner rushes for food delivery or opt for grocery delivery during more relaxed hours. The ability to select your availability means you can fit gig work into your existing schedule or use it as a primary source of income.

Navigating the Road Ahead

While ride-sharing and delivery services offer numerous benefits, such as flexibility and the potential for earnings, they come with their own set of challenges. These may include wear and tear on your vehicle, fuel costs, the need for excellent customer service, and navigating complex delivery routes.

Ride-sharing and delivery services offer a unique opportunity to transform your vehicle into a profit center. Whether you're looking for a flexible side hustle or considering it as a primary source of income, this chapter will equip you with the knowledge and tools needed to embark on your journey as a gig worker on the road.

4

Chapter 3: Clarifying Your Goals and Objectives

In the gig economy, setting clear goals and objectives is essential to ensure that your side hustle aligns with your financial aspirations and personal ambitions. In this chapter, we will explore the process of defining your goals, both short-term and long-term, and determining the crucial factors of how much you want to earn and the time frame in which you aim to achieve those goals.

Defining Short-Term and Long-Term Goals:

- Short-term goals: These are typically achievable within a year or less. They could include paying off a specific debt, saving for a vacation, or building an emergency fund.
- Long-term goals: These are aspirations that extend beyond a year and often shape your financial future. Examples include buying a home, funding your children's education, or retiring comfortably.

How Much Money Will You Need to Achieve Your Goal(s)?

- Calculate your financial needs: Determine the specific amount of money required to achieve each of your goals. Whether it's a down payment on a house or a target savings amount for retirement, having a clear figure in mind is crucial.
- Consider lifestyle factors: Think about the lifestyle you want to maintain or achieve. Your goals should align with your desired standard of living, which may impact the amount you need to earn.

How Long Will It Take To Reach Your Objective(s)?

- Short-term time frames: Decide when you want to achieve your short-term goals. Is it within the next six months, a year, or a few years? Setting a specific time frame provides a sense of urgency and focus.
- Long-term time frames: Long-term goals often require more extended periods for accomplishment. It could be 10, 20, or 30 years down the road. Establishing a realistic time frame ensures you have ample time to save and invest.
- Consider milestones: Break down long-term goals into smaller milestones to track your progress along the way. For example, if you're saving for retirement, set milestones for each decade leading up to it.

Aligning Your Side Hustle with Your Goals:

- Evaluate income potential: Assess the earning potential of your chosen side hustle and determine if it aligns with your financial goals. Will it help you reach your desired income target within the specified time frame?
- Adjust your side hustle strategy: Depending on your goals, you may need to fine-tune your approach to your side hustle. This might

involve taking on additional gigs, investing in skill development, or exploring new opportunities.

- Regularly review and adapt: Goals and circumstances change over time. Periodically review your goals and adjust them as needed. Your side hustle can evolve along with your aspirations.

5

Chapter 4: The Money Plan

Consider setting up a separate bank account for side hustle money. Financial organization is key to success. One effective strategy that can significantly enhance your financial management is the establishment of a separate bank account dedicated solely to your side hustle earnings. In this chapter, we'll delve into the importance of creating this distinct financial space and the numerous benefits it offers.

The Need for Separation:

As you embark on your gig work journey, it's crucial to recognize that your side hustle income, while supplemental to your primary source of income, deserves its own space in your financial landscape. Here's why:

1. Clarity and Transparency: Having a separate bank account helps you gain a clear view of your side hustle's financial health. Transactions are isolated, making it easier to track income and expenses specific to your gig work.
2. Effective Budgeting: A dedicated account simplifies budgeting. You can allocate funds for business-related expenses, taxes, savings,

and personal spending with greater precision.
3. Tax Compliance: Separating your side hustle income can make tax preparation less daunting. It ensures you have a clear record of your earnings, deductions, and expenses when tax season arrives.
4. Professionalism: A separate account lends an air of professionalism to your side hustle. It conveys a sense of dedication and responsibility to both clients and financial institutions.

Setting Up Your Dedicated Account:
Creating a separate bank account for your side hustle is a straightforward process. Follow these steps:

1. Choose the Right Bank: Research and select a reputable bank or financial institution that aligns with your needs. Look for low or no-fee business accounts, as these can be cost-effective for side hustlers.
2. Select the Right Account Type: You may wish to opt for a business account type that suits your gig work. Many banks offer business checking accounts specifically designed for small businesses and freelancers.
3. Provide Proper Documentation: Be prepared to provide necessary documentation, such as your Social Security number or Employer Identification Number (EIN), if applicable. Each bank has its requirements.
4. Keep Personal and Business Separate: Never mix personal and side hustle transactions in the same account. Deposit side hustle earnings into your dedicated account, and only use it for business-related expenses and savings.

The Benefits of Separation:
Now that you've established a separate bank account for your side

hustle, let's explore the tangible benefits it can bring to your financial life:

- Financial Clarity: With all side hustle transactions in one place, you can easily track income, expenses, and profits, allowing for better financial planning.
- Expense Tracking: Separating business expenses from personal ones simplifies expense tracking. You can readily identify deductible expenses for tax purposes.
- Tax Efficiency: At tax time, having a clean record of your side hustle income and expenses can streamline the tax filing process. You'll be well-prepared to claim deductions and meet your tax obligations.
- Savings and Investment: Your dedicated account can also serve as a savings vehicle. You can allocate a portion of your side hustle earnings for future goals or investments.
- Financial Organization: A separate account promotes financial organization and discipline, helping you maintain a professional and responsible approach to your gig work.

Maintaining Your Dedicated Account:

To fully reap the benefits of your separate bank account, it's essential to maintain good financial habits:

1. Regularly Review Transactions: Periodically review your account statements to ensure accuracy and identify areas for improvement in your financial management.
2. Set Aside for Taxes: Allocate a portion of your earnings to cover taxes. This proactive approach prevents a last-minute scramble to pay taxes owed.
3. Savings and Investment: Use the account to build savings for both short-term and long-term goals. Consider automating transfers

to your savings or investment accounts.
4. **Stay Within Budget:** Stick to your budget and avoid overspending from your side hustle account. Maintaining financial discipline is key to achieving your goals.

In conclusion, setting up a separate bank account for your side hustle earnings is a proactive and strategic move that can significantly enhance your financial organization and success. It provides clarity, simplifies budgeting, and ensures tax compliance, ultimately helping you achieve your financial goals while maintaining a professional image in the gig economy. With the right approach, your dedicated account becomes a valuable tool on your path to financial stability and prosperity in the world of side hustles.

Navigating the Tax Maze: Understanding Tax Implications for Gig Workers

Taxes are an inevitable part of life, and they apply to your gig work just as they do to any other source of income. However, gig workers face unique tax considerations that require careful attention and planning. In this chapter, we'll explore the tax implications that come with being a gig worker and provide guidance on how to navigate this often complex landscape.

Independent Contractor Status:

One of the defining features of gig work is the classification of gig workers as independent contractors rather than traditional employees. This distinction has significant tax implications:

- *Self-Employment Tax:* As an independent contractor, you are responsible for paying the full amount of Social Security and Medicare taxes, often referred to as self-employment taxes. This means you'll owe both the employer and employee portions of these taxes.

Tracking and Reporting Income:

Precise record-keeping is essential for gig workers. You should keep thorough records of all income earned, including earnings from multiple sources if you have multiple gigs. Key points to consider include:

- *Income Reporting:* Gig platforms may issue 1099 forms to report your income to the IRS if you earn over a certain threshold. However, you are still responsible for reporting all income, even if you don't receive a 1099.
- *Expense Deductions:* Keep records of any business-related expenses, as they can be deductible against your income. These might include vehicle expenses, home office expenses, and supplies necessary for your gig work.

Tax Credits and Deductions:

While gig workers face unique tax challenges, they also have access to various tax credits and deductions that can reduce their overall tax liability:

1. Home Office Deduction: If you use a portion of your home exclusively for your gig work, you may be eligible for a home office deduction, which can include expenses like rent or mortgage interest, utilities, and maintenance.
2. Business Mileage Deduction: If you use your vehicle for business-related purposes, you can deduct the cost of mileage driven for work. Maintaining a mileage log is crucial to substantiate this deduction.

3. Health Insurance Deduction: Self-employed gig workers may be eligible for a deduction on their health insurance premiums.

Seek Professional Guidance:

Navigating the tax implications of gig work can be complex, and the tax code is subject to change. Therefore, it's advisable to consult with a tax professional or accountant who specializes in self-employment and gig work.

While the tax implications of gig work may seem daunting, they are manageable with careful planning and attention to detail. By understanding the unique tax considerations for gig workers, keeping thorough records, and seeking professional guidance when needed, you can ensure that your gig work remains financially rewarding while staying in compliance with tax laws. Remember that staying informed and proactive is the key to a successful and stress-free tax season as a gig worker.

6

Chapter 5: The Good, The Bad and the Challenging Aspects of Gig Work

Pros

1. Flexibility: Choose Your Own Hours and Work on Your Terms

One of the most appealing aspects of gig work is the unmatched flexibility it offers. As a gig worker, you have the autonomy to craft your own work schedule, allowing you to strike a harmonious balance between your professional and personal life. Unlike traditional 9-to-5 jobs, you are not bound by fixed hours or rigid routines.

Whether you're a night owl, an early riser, or someone who thrives in the afternoon, gig work adapts to your preferred time frame. This flexibility caters to diverse lifestyles and commitments, making it ideal for students, parents, retirees, and anyone seeking supplementary income.

Furthermore, gig work grants you the liberty to determine the extent of your involvement. You can choose to work full-time, part-time, or sporadically, tailoring your efforts to meet your financial goals and lifestyle aspirations. This unparalleled freedom empowers you to seize control of your work-life balance, making gig work a versatile and adaptable option for income generation.

2. Tips: Unlocking Extra Earnings from Satisfied Customers

In the gig economy, one rewarding perk is the potential to receive tips from appreciative customers. This additional income can significantly boost your overall earnings and create a positive incentive for exceptional service. Whether you're delivering food, providing rides, or offering freelance services, going the extra mile can lead to generous tips.

Satisfying customers by delivering quality, timeliness, and excellent communication often results in gratuities that add up over time. These tips not only enhance your immediate income but also encourage repeat business and positive reviews, ultimately amplifying your gig work success. Embracing a customer-centric approach can transform occasional tips into a reliable stream of additional revenue, making gig work even more financially rewarding. So, remember, exceptional service doesn't just earn you gratitude—it also puts extra money in your pocket.

3. Variety: Embrace Diversity in Interactions and Locations

Gig work offers a vibrant tapestry of experiences enriched by variety. By engaging in gig activities, you open doors to diverse encounters with people from all walks of life and opportunities to explore various locations. Whether you're a rideshare driver, a delivery person, or a freelancer, your work is a dynamic journey.

Interacting with a multitude of personalities and backgrounds enriches your interpersonal skills and broadens your horizons. Each day presents a unique chance to connect, learn, and share experiences. Additionally, gig work often takes you to different places, neighborhoods, or even cities, adding a touch of adventure to your professional life.

This delightful variety infuses excitement into your gig work, making it an engaging and ever-evolving experience. It's a reminder that the gig economy isn't just about earning—it's about embracing the colorful tapestry of human interaction and the thrill of exploring new landscapes.

4. Side Hustle Weekly or Daily Pay: Consistent Financial Flow

One of the alluring features of side hustles is the ability to access regular income on a weekly or daily basis. Unlike traditional jobs with fixed monthly paychecks, gig work often allows you to receive your earnings more frequently. This consistent financial flow offers a sense of stability and immediacy, which can be particularly valuable when dealing with financial goals or unexpected expenses.

The prospect of getting paid weekly or daily provides a steady stream of income, making it easier to manage day-to-day finances and respond to immediate needs. This flexibility empowers gig workers to adapt their financial strategies to their unique circumstances, whether it's covering bills, saving for goals, or simply enjoying the peace of mind that comes with regular earnings. Side hustle pay frequency aligns with the fast-paced nature of the gig economy, offering convenience and financial security to those who embrace it.

5. Independent Contractor Status: Empowerment and Tax Advantages

Gig work often designates you as an independent contractor, granting you greater autonomy and control over your work. This status enables you to set your own schedules, choose clients, and even dictate your work methods. Additionally, it comes with potential tax benefits, allowing you to deduct certain business-related expenses, which can lead to significant savings during tax season. This independent contractor status not only fosters a sense of empowerment but also provides financial advantages for savvy gig workers, making it a sought-after feature of the gig economy.

6. Accessibility: Work Virtually Anywhere, Anytime

Gig work transcends geographical boundaries, offering the remarkable advantage of accessibility. You can embark on your gig journey from virtually anywhere, be it the heart of a bustling city or the quiet tranquility of a rural town. The gig economy's wide reach ensures that opportunities are accessible to a diverse range of individuals, regardless of their location. All you need is an internet connection or a mode of transportation, depending on your gig type. This accessibility democratizes income generation, making gig work a viable option for those seeking to leverage their skills, assets, or resources, no matter where they call home, and granting them the freedom to work on their own terms.

7. Multi-Tasking: Enhancing Efficiency Through Entertainment

Certain gig work roles grant a unique advantage: the ability to multitask while working. Whether you're delivering goods, performing data entry, or conducting online tasks, many gig workers have the flexibility to enjoy audiobooks, stay updated with the latest news, or groove to music playlists. This fusion of productivity and entertainment not only makes the workday more enjoyable but also enhances overall efficiency. It transforms mundane tasks into engaging opportunities to expand your knowledge, stay informed, or simply savor your favorite tunes, illustrating how gig work can seamlessly integrate with your personal interests and preferences.

CONS

1. Inconsistent Income: Reliance on Tips Leads to Fluctuating

Earnings
One notable challenge in gig work is the unpredictability of income. Many gig workers rely heavily on tips, which can vary significantly from one job to another. This reliance on gratuities means that earnings may fluctuate, making it challenging to predict or stabilize income. While tips can substantially boost earnings, the inconsistency can be a financial concern for those seeking a steady and reliable source of income.

2. Vehicle Costs: Navigating the Wear and Tear
For gig workers who rely on their own vehicles, an often underestimated factor is the wear and tear inflicted on their cars. Constant use for deliveries, ridesharing, or other gig-related tasks can accelerate vehicle depreciation, increase maintenance needs, and elevate fuel expenses.

Regularly assessing your vehicle's condition and maintenance requirements is essential. Budgeting for oil changes, tire replacements, and unexpected repairs can help you manage these costs effectively. Additionally, fuel expenses can add up, so optimizing your routes and driving habits can make a noticeable difference.

Understanding the true cost of vehicle use in gig work is crucial for financial planning. While the convenience of using your car is undeniable, it's essential to weigh the expenses against the income generated to ensure that gig work remains a viable and financially sustainable option.

3. Stress: The Physically and Mentally Demanding Side of the Side Hustle
While side hustles offer financial opportunities, they can also introduce a unique set of stressors. The relentless demands of managing your primary job, personal life, and gig work can take a toll on your well-being.

Physically Demanding: Some side hustles, like physical labor, delivery services, or event staffing, require strenuous physical effort. The constant movement and manual labor can lead to exhaustion and even physical strain or injury.

Mentally Taxing: Other side hustles, such as freelance writing, graphic design, or virtual assistance, can be mentally taxing due to tight deadlines, client expectations, and the pressure to consistently deliver high-quality work.

Balancing these demands can be challenging, impacting your work-life balance and potentially straining personal relationships. However, recognizing these stressors is the first step in managing them effectively. Setting clear boundaries, practicing time management, and prioritizing self-care can help mitigate the stress associated with juggling a side hustle alongside other commitments.

4. No Guaranteed Hours: Variable Earnings and No Minimum Wage (State-Dependent)

Gig workers typically face the absence of guaranteed hours, which means there's no assurance of a minimum wage or set number of work hours. The flexibility of gig work comes with the trade-off of income inconsistency, as earnings can fluctuate significantly based on factors like demand, location, and job availability. It's essential for gig workers to adapt to this dynamic nature of gig work and plan accordingly to ensure financial stability. Minimum wage regulations vary by state, further influencing income potential in the gig economy.

5. Customer Complaints: Managing Frustration and Time-Consuming Resolutions

In the gig economy, dealing with customer complaints is an inevitable aspect of the job. These grievances can range from missing or damaged items in deliveries to service dissatisfaction in various gig roles. Resolving these issues can be time-consuming and emotionally draining, as maintaining a positive reputation often hinges on effective complaint resolution. The need to balance customer satisfaction with personal well-being can create added stress for gig workers, highlighting the importance of patience and effective communication.

Handling difficult clients in gig work involves patience, active listening, and professionalism. Address their concerns promptly, offer solutions, and maintain clear communication to resolve issues and maintain a positive reputation.

6. Limited Benefits: The Absence of Traditional Employee Perks

One significant downside of gig work is the absence of traditional employee benefits that come with regular employment. Gig workers typically don't receive benefits such as health insurance, paid time off, retirement plans, or employer-sponsored perks like gym memberships or commuter benefits.

This lack of benefits can be particularly challenging for gig workers who rely solely on gig income for their livelihood. The responsibility for securing health coverage, saving for retirement, and managing time off rests squarely on their shoulders. It can also lead to financial insecurity during periods of illness or when a break from work is needed.

Navigating these limitations requires gig workers to proactively seek alternative solutions, such as purchasing individual health insurance plans, setting up personal retirement accounts, and budgeting for unpaid time off. While gig work offers flexibility, the trade-off is the need to manage and plan for these essential aspects of financial well-being independently.

7. Competition: Navigating the Crowded Marketplace (Be The G.O.A.T.)

In the world of side hustles, competition can be cutthroat, particularly in densely populated or urban areas. The proliferation of gig workers vying for similar opportunities can lead to oversaturation in certain markets. This heightened competition may affect your ability to secure orders, clients, or gigs consistently.

To thrive in such environments, side hustlers often need to differentiate themselves by offering exceptional service, leveraging their unique skills, or exploring niche markets. Be the Greatest Of All Time in your area! Additionally, staying updated with market trends and adapting to changing demand can help you remain competitive and carve out your space in the crowded marketplace of side hustles.

8. Dependence on App Ratings: Shaping Your Gig Work Opportunities

Your app ratings and reviews wield significant influence over your ability to secure orders and clients. Positive ratings can open doors to many more opportunities, while negative feedback can limit your gig work prospects. However, these ratings can be subjective and may not always reflect your performance accurately. Navigating this dependence on app ratings requires consistently providing excellent service and addressing customer concerns promptly to maintain a positive reputation and secure a steady flow of orders.

7

Chapter 6: Work Smarter, Not Harder

To excel in your side hustle and make it a sustainable source of income, several key strategies and practices can be instrumental in your journey to success. It all begins with prioritizing effective time management, as this ensures that you allocate sufficient time and effort to your side hustle amidst your other commitments. Setting clear and achievable goals is paramount; these objectives will serve as your guiding stars, helping you stay focused and motivated. A strong work ethic is the foundation of any thriving side hustle, instilling discipline and dedication into your work routine.

Additionally, consider leveraging your unique skills and interests to carve a niche in the gig economy. Conduct thorough research to gauge market demand and identify opportunities where your talents align. Creating a reliable schedule that balances your various responsibilities is essential for maintaining consistency and meeting deadlines.

Integrating productivity tools into your workflow can boost efficiency and help you manage tasks more effectively. Strong communication skills, coupled with top-notch customer service, can set you apart from the competition, fostering client trust and loyalty. Embrace the challenge of handling difficult clients with professionalism, using such

CHAPTER 6: WORK SMARTER, NOT HARDER

experiences as opportunities for growth.

Remember that seeking support when faced with challenges or uncertainty is a sign of wisdom, not weakness. Connect with fellow gig workers or mentors who can provide guidance and insights based on their experiences.

Lastly, continuous adaptation and refinement of your approach are essential to remain competitive and aligned with evolving market trends. By staying flexible and open to change, you can better position yourself to achieve your financial goals and flourish in the dynamic world of side hustles.

8

Conclusion

Embarking on a journey in gig work can be both exciting and daunting, especially when facing self-doubt and fear. However, remember that every successful gig worker was once in your shoes. Here are some final words of encouragement:

- **Start Small:** Begin with gigs that align with your skills and interests. Starting small allows you to build confidence gradually.
- **Embrace Learning:** Gig work is a learning experience. Don't fear making mistakes; view them as opportunities for growth.
- **Set Realistic Expectations:** Understand that success may not be immediate. Be patient with yourself and stay committed to improvement.
- **Network:** Connect with other gig workers to gain insights and support. They've likely faced similar challenges.
- **Celebrate Wins:** Even small accomplishments deserve recognition. Celebrate your achievements, no matter how minor they may seem.
- **Self-Care:** Prioritize self-care to manage stress and maintain a healthy work-life balance.
- **Stay Persistent:** Perseverance is key. Overcoming self-doubt and

CONCLUSION

fear is a journey, but it's one that leads to personal and financial growth.

- ***Take a Day Off:*** In gig work, taking a day off occasionally is crucial for recharging, preventing burnout, and maintaining both physical and mental well-being.

Remember, every gig worker was once new to the game, and the gig economy offers a world of opportunities for those who dare to overcome their doubts and fears. Your potential for success is boundless, so take that first step and embrace the adventure ahead!

Made in United States
Orlando, FL
09 February 2024